Dear Parent:
Your child's love of reading starts here!

Every child learns to read in a different way and at his or her own speed. Some go back and forth between reading levels and read favorite books again and again. Others read through each level in order. You can help your young reader improve and become more confident by encouraging his or her own interests and abilities. From books your child reads with you to the first books he or she reads alone, there are I Can Read Books for every stage of reading:

SHARED READING
Basic language, word repetition, and whimsical illustrations, ideal for sharing with your emergent reader

BEGINNING READING
Short sentences, familiar words, and simple concepts for children eager to read on their own

READING WITH HELP
Engaging stories, longer sentences, and language play for developing readers

READING ALONE
Complex plots, challenging vocabulary, and high-interest topics for the independent reader

ADVANCED READING
Short paragraphs, chapters, and exciting themes for the perfect bridge to chapter books

I Can Read Books have introduced children to the joy of reading since 1957. Featuring award-winning authors and illustrators and a fabulous cast of beloved characters, I Can Read Books set the standard for beginning readers.

A lifetime of discovery begins with the magical words **"I Can Read!"**

Visit www.icanread.com for information
on enriching your child's reading experience.

For Patrick and Emma
—S.K.

I dedicate this book to
my friends: Ryan, Claire,
Dylan, and Keegan.
—G.M.

Picture Credits

The following photographs, paintings, and engravings are © Getty Images:
page 26, Ben Franklin's Print Press, GraphicaArtis; Ben Franklin lightning painting, Universal History Archive; page 27, Ben Franklin standing before the Lords in Council in Whitehall Chapel, Universal History Archive; Signing of the US Constitution, Bettmann; page 28, printing press used by Ben Franklin, Ipsumpix; title page of *Poor Richard's Almanack* for 1740, Bettmann; page 29, Ben Franklin's stove invention, Werner Wolf; Ben Franklin's bifocal invention, Bettmann; page 30, Benjamin Franklin's Electrical Machine, Kean Collection; Lightning conductor, c. 1749, Science & Society Picture Library; page 31, portrait of Ben Franklin in a fur hat, DEA Picture Library; Constitution of the United States, Fine Art; US Declaration of Independence, Hulton Archive; page 32, Benjamin Franklin portrait by David Martin, Fine Art.
The following images are reproduced courtesy of the Library of Congress:
page 28, page of the *Pennsylvania Gazette*, May 9, 1754; page 29, leaf print money; page 31, the Treaty of Paris.

I Can Read Book® is a trademark of HarperCollins Publishers.

Ben Franklin Thinks Big
Copyright © 2018 by HarperCollins Publishers
All rights reserved. Manufactured in China.
No part of this book may be used or reproduced in any manner whatsoever without written permission except in the case of brief quotations embodied in critical articles and reviews. For information address HarperCollins Children's Books, a division of HarperCollins Publishers, 195 Broadway, New York, NY 10007.
www.icanread.com

Library of Congress Control Number: 2018933323
ISBN 978-0-06-243264-3 (trade bdg.) — ISBN 978-0-06-243263-6 (pbk.)

Book design by Celeste Knudsen

18 19 20 21 22 SCP 10 9 8 7 6 5 4 3 2 1

❖   First Edition

I Can Read!™

READING
2
WITH HELP

BEN FRANKLIN
Thinks Big

story by Sheila Keenan
pictures by Gustavo Mazali

HARPER

An Imprint of HarperCollinsPublishers

"What good shall I do today?"
Benjamin Franklin always asked.
His answers changed the world!

Ben thought working hard,
learning, and doing good were
the most important things in life.
That's how he became
a famous writer and inventor
and helped the thirteen colonies
become the United States.

At ten, Ben already had a job.

By day, he made candles

for his father's shop in Boston.

By night, he burned candles

and stayed up reading.

Ben learned many things from books,

even how to swim!

He was a very curious person

who loved to test out ideas.

Young Ben went to work
for his older brother James.
He learned to be a printer.
Ben stopped eating meat.
He spent the money he saved
on books.

Ben secretly wrote for James's
newspaper under a fake name.
Readers loved his clever writing.
But James did not like being fooled.
The Franklin brothers argued.
So Ben struck out on his own.

When Franklin was twenty-two,
he opened his own print shop
in Philadelphia.
Ben used a squeaky wheelbarrow
to make deliveries.
People could tell how hard he worked;
they heard him coming!

Ben married Deborah Read.

He wrote news stories
and worked the heavy printing press.
Deborah ran the busy shop.

Ben Franklin became
the most successful printer
in the colonies.
People from New York to Virginia
read his weekly newspaper,
the *Pennsylvania Gazette*.

Ben published a bestselling book
called *Poor Richard's Almanack*,
and it made him rich.
Ben didn't just print
books and papers.
He also printed money
for Pennsylvania and other colonies!

Ben believed in helping make life
better for everybody.
He looked around to see
what people needed.
Franklin helped form Philadelphia's
first firefighting group,
the first general hospital,
and the first lending library
in the country.
As he wrote, "Well done is better
than well said."

Ben Franklin really loved
to invent things, too.
Was your fireplace working poorly?
Ben's invention the Franklin stove
sent heat into a room
and sent smoke up the chimney.

Were the streetlights dim?

Franklin's new square lights glowed.

Ben retired from printing

to study science full-time.

He made a shocking discovery!

Ben Franklin discovered the link

between lightning and electricity.

He flew a kite into a stormy sky.

The kite was zapped by lightning!

An electrical charge

struck the kite's metal tip,

traveled down a string,

hit a key—and gave Ben a shock.

Ben then invented the lightning rod.

Lightning bolts struck the iron rod

instead of the roof.

That stopped buildings from burning.

Franklin's discoveries made him
famous around the world.
He was also a member
of the government in Pennsylvania.
Ben was sent to London to ask
for more rights for the colonies.
He was not successful.
Still, he stayed there for many years.

Then the Revolutionary War started.

The American colonists

were fighting the British.

Franklin sailed home.

He studied the ocean along the way.

Once home, Franklin helped write
the Declaration of Independence.
Then Franklin sailed to France
to ask for money and soldiers
for the war against the British.

Ben got the French
to help America win the war.
He worked out a peace treaty
with England.
Ben was gone for nine years.
He met royalty and scientists
and invented bifocal eyeglasses!

Ben Franklin returned

to what was now the United States.

He was nearly eighty,

but he still served

as the leader of Pennsylvania.

He helped write

the new country's constitution.

And he lived at home with his family.

Ben Franklin died in his bed,

true to his own words:

"Wish not so much to live long,

as to live well."

Timeline

1706
Franklin is born on January 17, in Boston, Massachusetts.

1718
Franklin is apprenticed to his brother James, a printe

1723
Franklin runs away to New York, then Philadelphia.

1728
Franklin opens "Ben J. Franklin Printer and Bookseller."

1729
Franklin starts publishing the *Pennsylvania Gazette*.

1730
Deborah Read becomes Franklin's wife.

1732
Franklin first publishes *Poor Richard's Almanack*.

1741
Franklin invents the Franklin stove.

1752
Franklin conducts the kite experiment.

1753
Franklin publishes his invention of the lightning rod in *Poor Richard's Almanack*.

Timeline (continued)

1757
Franklin goes abroad, mainly in England, and represents Pennsylvania and other colonies.

1774
Franklin's wife, Deborah, dies.

1775
The Revolutionary War begins. Franklin returns to America.

1776
Franklin helps write the Declaration of Independence and travels to France.

1779–81
Franklin negotiates peace treaty with England.

1783
Franklin signs peace treaty, the Treaty of Paris, that ends the Revolutionary War.

1784
Franklin invents bifocals.

1785
Franklin is elected the leader of Pennsylvania.

1787
Franklin helps write and signs the US Constitution.

1790
Franklin dies on April 17.

Benjamin Franklin's early career was all about printing and writing.

Ben Franklin's printing press

This is Ben Franklin's newspaper, the *Pennsylvania Gazette*.

Poor Richard's Almanack was a small popular almanac that came out every year. It had a calendar and useful facts, dates, jokes, riddles, and witty sayings. Franklin also created a character for his almanac. People bought it to find out what happened next to "Poor Richard."

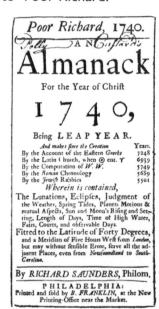

Like many founding fathers, Franklin was a slave owner. His newspaper ran ads about slave sales. (At the same time, he printed pamphlets *against* slavery for the Quakers, a religious group who opposed slavery.)

Later, Franklin changed his thinking about slavery and spoke out against it. He became an abolitionist—a person who wanted to end slavery.

Ben Franklin was an enthusiastic inventor.

His inventions included the Franklin stove, bifocal glasses, and a special way to print money using leaf prints. This money could not be counterfeited (faked)!

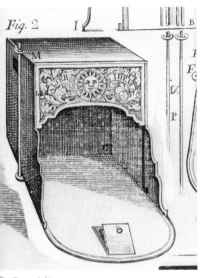

A Franklin stove

Franklin's bifocals

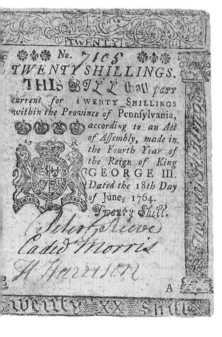

Franklin's colonial leaf print money

Ben Franklin conducted many experiments with electricity.

These experiments helped Ben's understanding that lightning was electricity.

This is Ben Franklin's electrical machine invention which makes static energy by rubbing a leather pad against a spinning glass globe to make an electrical charge in the glass globe.

Primera máquina eléctrica de Franklin

Benjamin Franklin invented the lightning rod.

Here's a replica of Ben Franklin's lightning rod. It helped protect people and buildings from lightning. Franklin believed the lightning rod was his most important invention.

Ben Franklin became famous.

His groundbreaking discoveries made Franklin famous outside America. When he went to France in 1776 he was a big celebrity. He was known as a scientist, but he was also known for his hat! Franklin wore a fur hat on his trip to keep his head warm. But to the French, he looked like a rugged American frontiersman. He ordered more hats!

Ben Franklin signed the most important documents in US history.

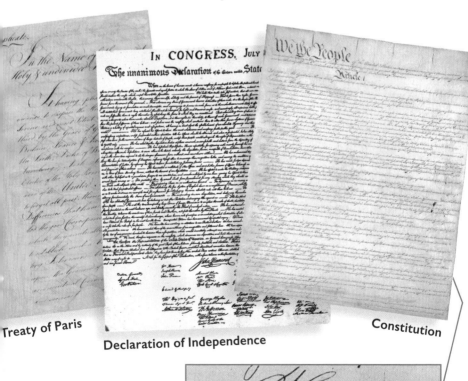

Treaty of Paris

Declaration of Independence

Constitution

Franklin's signature on fourth page of the Constitution

This portrait by David Martin hangs in the White House.

Ben Franklin once wrote:
"If you would not be forgotten
as soon as you are dead and rotten,
either write things worth reading
or do things worth the writing."

Ben did both!